Contents

Introduction

We love our pets and want to take good care of them, nevertheless, many rabbit owners still make mistakes in feeding their little rascals. Of course, they don't make those mistakes intentionally – very few people would deliberately harm their animals. They are made out of unawareness, because even if you make an effort and inform yourself, you still come across a lot of misinformation, which is spread in pet shops, on the internet and even in guidebooks!

Especially the staff in the pet shop is usually trusted, as it is their profession and they must know their way around. However, unfortunately, this is usually not the case, as pet shops want to sell their industrial dry food and could not make a profit with species-appropriate nutrition. For this reason, customers are also being enticed to buy the cute baby rabbits or puppies on sale – and not out of love for animals. Once the rabbit or puppy is sold, supplies are immediately procured by the pet shop. Unfortunately, in most cases these supplies come from dubious breeders who treat animals like merchandise and usually keep them under inadequate conditions.

Do not blame yourself, if you have also fed your animals (partially) foreign foods to their species. There are simply too many dubious sources out there. I have been a pet owner for almost thirty years and have unfortunately made several mistakes over the years because I was simply misinformed. I followed the guidebooks of that time, which also recommended keeping animals in small cages. It was also hardly discussed that wild rabbits live in colonies and need at least one animal friend of the same species. Sadly, that's how it was for decades - fortunately, we know better today!

But before we really get started: product reviews are the basis for the success of independent authors. For this reason, I would be very grateful for feedback on this guide in the form of a review. In your review, please let me know how you liked the book. If you don't have time for this, you can alternatively just award stars without providing a written review. A few words would be great, of course. But no matter if it's short or long: with your opinion or your star rating you help both future readers and me as a writer! Thank you.

And now, let us begin!

The physiology of rabbits

We all know for certain that rabbits are not carnivores or omnivores. Rabbits are pure herbivores, just like about 90% of all mammals. However, rabbits belong to a very special type of herbivore: They are folivores! That means that they are mainly leaf-eaters.

The teeth of rabbits are designed to grind and crush the plant food. Rabbits can move their jaw sideways and accordingly grind their food before swallowing it. The same applies to humans. Herein lies a big difference to the carnivore (lion, cat, etc.), because the carnivore has fangs and sharp molars, with which it cuts up its prey and swallows it in large pieces, almost without any chewing.

This is another reason why it is essential that rabbits are well occupied with chewing their food. Anyone who has ever eaten grass knows how rich it is in raw fibre, because you must chew grass for (what feels like) an endless amount of time to finally swallow it. Such long, perpetual and intensive chewing is very important for the preservation of the rabbit's molars. Otherwise, sooner or later serious dental problems may occur because the teeth of rabbits grow continuously.

Through intensive chewing, the upper and lower molars grind each other. If the teeth become too long, rabbits can be extremely hindered in eating and the veterinarian may even have to file the teeth.

If you already have rabbits and are not just about to buy them for the first time, you have probably already noticed how often rabbits eat and how much they poop accordingly. This is another reason why it is so important not to humanise rabbits. Humans and rabbits differ tremendously in this respect!

People eat on average two to four times a day and go "for number two" on average once a day. People can even go without solid food for weeks and come out of fasting completely healthy (or healthier!).

Rabbits, on the other hand, feed up to 80 (!) times a day. This is not a sign of gluttony, but quite normal. They also defecate very often during the day and excrete the "waste" of their body bit by bit.

By the way, the same applies to their sleeping habits: while most humans sleep once a day and have a long sleeping period (usually six to eight hours), rabbits do not have such long sleep phases. They nap more often than humans, but also much shorter. The sleep-eat-poo phases simply occur much more often in rabbits than in humans.

Another special feature is that rabbits produce the so-called "cecum poops". As in humans, the rabbit's food passes from the mouth into the stomach and then into the small intestine. But the rabbit has another station: the cecum appendix. This is where vitamins and nutrients are processed.

Cecum poop is often eaten by rabbits - this is normal and healthy. You should only worry if a rabbit eats a noticeable amount of excrement. This can be a sign that the rabbit is not getting enough nutrients from its food and that he/she needs to "get" them elsewhere. Or the rabbit might have an increased need in nutrients due to a disease!

Incidentally, if you feed your rabbits a species-appropriate diet, you don't have to worry about them gaining weight and becoming fat - even if they eat greens without limitation. Animals that are fed properly do not become overweight.

Only humans get fat, because some people unfortunately shovel more and more "garbage" into their bodies, and their eating habits often come close to gluttony. The only animals that are or become overweight are incorrectly fed domestic pets - and this is only due to the inadequate feeding methods of pet owners. Hence, there are no fat animals in the wild, as wild animals instinctively feed themselves in a species-appropriate way and consume what they need.

Sourcing species appropriate food

It doesn't need to be expensive to keep rabbits as pets. In fact, caring for rabbits can be extremely inexpensive if the animals are fed properly. Well, of course it can always happen that an animal falls ill and needs to be treated by a vet. Such a treatment can be very expensive, depending on the illness, and in the worst case the animal may even need an operation - so you should always have saved enough money to be prepared for such cases! But apart from that, rabbit keeping (or keeping most small animals in general) is very inexpensive if you obtain the animal food mainly from nature. Nature provides us with everything that our animals need to be fully nourished.

Of course, it is important in which area you live. Some people are lucky enough to have their own garden with lots of grass and many wild herbs. Other people live near a forest, where you can also find many kinds of trees, grasses and wild herbs.

But not everyone is that lucky - and that is fine. Just because you may not have much nature around you does not mean that you cannot keep rabbits. You don't have to offer every plant species to your pets if the possibility simply doesn't exist.

However, there are often more possibilities than you might realise at first. Think about where you could find suitable trees, grasses and wild herbs in your area - or ask around. It's also a good idea to contact your council first and ask them if you are allowed to collect plants for your rabbits in the area.

Since rabbit food usually consists of plants which grow in the wild en masse, this is usually not a problem. Grass, dandelions, daisies, ribwort, clover and so on can usually be found in abundance. Of course, we leave ornamental plants, which are planted by the city in parks and forests, alone.

The best possibilities for gathering food are offered by forests, as you can usually find all kinds of trees and large meadows in there. Otherwise, you could ask friends and relatives with gardens if you can pick rabbit food from their garden. I'm sure they will be happy to help you.

Nearby farmers are also often happy to help - but you should not touch their hayfields, as they use them to make hay which they either use for their own animals or sell. You can also collect from the roadside if the roads are not too busy. However, you should wash this food well because of the exhaust fumes. You might also collect food for your rabbits in parks, by lakes, ponds and along field paths - if this is not prohibited.

A lot of food for rabbits grows at the pond or lake.

In the park you may also collect food if allowed.

If you want to collect food from friends, family or farmers, please make sure that no poisons (such as rat poison or similar) are being used there.

Once you have collected the food, it is usually unnecessary to wash it before feeding. In the wild, rabbits eat the plants unwashed, so this is usually not a problem. Furthermore, rabbits have a much better olfactory organ than, for example, humans - so dirty food is normally left lying around anyway. Even if, for example, a dog has urinated on the plants, rabbits usually do not eat them because they are not edible. This is another reason why it is so important that rabbits always have more than enough food at their disposal. They should be given the opportunity to choose and select the best parts of the food. Therefore, the animals should not be forced to eat all of it before you give them more.

Along field paths you can usually also find great green fodder.

Hay

It is essential that your rabbits always have access to hay. Hay consists mainly of dried grasses. This is very often enriched with dried herbs. As hay has a very high raw fibre content, it must be chewed very well and thoroughly, but does not provide too many calories.

Under ideal conditions rabbits would feed exclusively on leaves, grasses, herbs and other plants. However, this is not always possible and not every country in the world offers the perfect conditions. Especially in northern regions it is often difficult to provide rabbits with fresh food from nature all year round. For this reason, hay can be a good substitute.

The subject of 'tooth abrasion' is often discussed - and rightly so, as this is one of the most important issues when it comes to keeping rabbits in a species appropriate way. First, you should be aware that the small body of a rabbit functions quite differently than, for example, the human body. While humans lose their first teeth and keep the second set of teeth for life, rabbits' teeth grow continuously. Human teeth retain a certain length and if a tooth breaks off or is lost, it will not grow back. This is different with rabbits. To prevent rabbits' teeth from becoming too long, they must constantly rub against each other.

Unfortunately, it is a myth that hard food is needed to wear down the teeth. Therefore, many people feed hard bread, breadsticks etc. to their rabbits. However, this is not optimal and probably even harmful, as these foods soften quickly in combination with saliva, and they satiate for a very long time. The rabbit therefore eats less, and the teeth do not rub against each other. The teeth do not primarily rub off on the food itself, but on the opposite teeth – tooth abrasion is therefore supported by eating a lot of food rich in crude fibre, which does not satiate for too long. These are leaves, herbs and grasses.

If the teeth become too long, this can be very hindering when eating. In the worst case, the vet will have to file the teeth and serious digestive problems may occur.

When rabbits get fresh food from meadows and trees, they often do not pay much attention to their hay. If there is a choice between fresh food and dry hay, most animals choose fresh food. This is perfectly normal. Nevertheless, hay should always be offered as a supplement and alternative. The same applies to fresh water: even if rabbits cover their water requirements by eating fresh food, additional water should always be offered.

Rabbits are true gourmets and usually pick out the best parts of the food. It is therefore not unusual for rabbits not to eat all the hay offered, but to leave a remainder. They pick out the best and most valuable hay straws and are therefore dependent on fresh hay being given to them daily. Therefore, you should not wait until all the hay has been eaten before there is a hay replenishment for your rabbits.

Although there are more than two hundred types of grasses, only a few of them are used to produce hay. Often about two to twelve different types of grass are used for hay production. Commonly used are cocksfoot, meadow grass or ryegrass.

Please make sure that you always keep the hay for your rabbits in a dry place. Hay should not come into contact with moisture and should ideally be stored in the dark. Perfect storage is in a wooden box, cardboard box or cloth bag. Plastic packaging is unsuitable for storage, as plastic is impermeable to air.

Grass

Rabbits are primarily leaf-eaters. There is a small but subtle difference to some other small domestic pets!

A good example is the guinea pig. The diet of rabbits and guinea pigs is very similar. The same applies to the physiology of the two species, because they are similar in this respect as well. Both species eat grass as well as leaves and wild herbs, but grass is the main food for guinea pigs, while leafy plants are the main food for rabbits. The foods are therefore basically the same, but the amount of each feed varies. Rabbits usually prioritise leafy plants, guinea pigs prioritise grasses.

Grass should ideally be plucked by hand or cut with garden shears. You should not feed mown grass, as it immediately starts to ferment. If you feed plucked grass or grass cut with shears, feeding it the next day is usually not a problem either, as the grass ferments more slowly.

Wet grass can also be fed without any problem, as rabbits also feed on rain-soaked food in the wild. Therefore, the myth that wet greens should not be fed is not true. However, it should be noted that wet grass usually ferments faster than dry grass. Therefore, you should ideally pass it on to your rabbits immediately.

Especially in hot summer months, plucked or cut grass does not last too long. Your rabbits should therefore eat it the same day. Often the grass is already half dried out the next day and curls partially – in that case it is no longer a safe food.

Wild herbs

Finding wild herbs can be more difficult than finding simple grass but is feasible in most areas. It depends on in which area you live. A large selection of herbs is ideal, so that rabbits can pick out exactly what they need. Rabbits, like many other animals, are experts at picking out the food their small bodies require at any given moment.

Some plants - such as dandelions, daisies and nettles - are found almost everywhere. But other wild plants are also easy to identify. Often people don't pay much attention to the plants they are surrounded by every day.

Let us take a closer look at the most common wild plants on the following pages!

Dandelions

Dandelions are extremely popular with most rabbits, and rightly so. Especially the leaves of dandelions are very popular, but the flower and stem can also be fed.

Dandelions are very high in provitamin A. In addition, vitamin C is also abundant - about 67,778 micrograms per 100 grams! Although rabbits can also produce vitamin C themselves, dandelions are an extremely healthy herb, and both rabbits and humans can benefit from its positive effects.

Vitamin C is produced in the rabbit's liver and/or absorbed by eating "cecum poop". Excess vitamin C is excreted through the urine.

Humans are dependent on an external supply of vitamin C through food since humans cannot produce this vitamin themselves. This also applies to the guinea pig - which is also a very popular pet.

A myth about dandelions says that it promotes calcium deposits and leads to urinary and kidney stones. It is also said to promote bladder slime. Allegedly, the dandelion's calcium should be responsible for this. However, this is not true if a rabbit is fed in a species-appropriate way!

The diseases listed above do not usually occur when a rabbit is fed mainly on herbs, leaves, grass and vegetables. Due to the high fluid intake with such a species-appropriate diet, the small rabbit body is always well "flushed" and excretes excess calcium simply through the urine.

Therefore, it can also happen that a rabbit gives off whitish urine. This is not a cause for concern, as it is simply a sign that excess calcium has been flushed out. Therefore, you do not need to be worried.

However, a problem can arise if rabbits eat too much dry food. Pellets and (cereal) dry food are to blame here. This food is extremely foreign to the species and no rabbit needs it. In the wild, rabbits feed on fresh food and do not consume dry food, especially not industrial food.

With such a diet it is quite possible that a rabbit does not take up enough water, and calcium accumulates in the body. The same is true for salt lickstones - salt removes additional water from the body.

Furthermore, a rabbit absorbs all minerals it needs through fresh food, if a good and large selection is provided. An additional administration of minerals or vitamins is not necessary with a species-appropriate diet if the rabbit does not have any particular diseases.

Furthermore, dandelions can have a diuretic effect and thus also help to "flush" the body well.

Nettles

The stinging nettle is probably not one of the most popular plants, as probably everyone has come into contact with it at least once in their life. Once you have "burned" yourself on it, you probably give it a wide berth. Incidentally, nettles are extremely healthy! Like dandelions, nettles have a diuretic effect and cleanse the blood.

Stinging nettles provide important minerals such as iron and magnesium, but also a high dose of vitamin C (about 333,000 micrograms per 100 grams). They are also a valuable source of various B vitamins, vitamin A and vitamin E.

Nettles

The small hairs on the nettle can cause pain and wheals on the skin. However, there is a simple trick to make nettles "harmless" - if you pull the nettle plant through your hand from bottom to top, the tips of the small burning hairs break off and the plant no longer hurts. As a precaution, this is best done with gloves. It is also advisable to do the procedure three or four times to make sure that you have caught all the hair tips.

However, even if you hurt yourself at the tips of the hairs, this is no reason to worry. It is not dangerous; it just burns a little. You don't have to worry about your rabbits either, as they don't get hurt by nettles. They can even eat them without hurting themselves – lucky animals!

Stinging nettles don't always have to be fed very fresh but can be a little wilted. Experience shows that wilted nettles are even preferred by some rabbits.

Daisies

Daisies are not only pretty, but also very healthy. The small flowers contain many important bitter substances and flavonoids. These substances strengthen the immune system of your rabbits and also have an antioxidant effect. In addition, daisies are also good sources of vitamin A, vitamin C, vitamin E, iron, potassium and magnesium.

Furthermore, daisies have a blood-purifying and digestive effect. They also stimulate the metabolism. All these advantages make daisies an ideal food for rabbits! The whole plant can be fed, especially the flower.

Daisies

Camomile

The camomile plant is probably known mainly due to camomile tea. As children, many of us were given camomile tea for stomach aches. The plant behind it is considered a medicinal plant and tastes good - not only to humans, but also to rabbits!

Camomile can help with digestive problems and stomach aches and alleviate the discomfort. The plant grows mainly between May and September and is mostly found on fallow land or in fields.

Due to the flavonoids contained in the camomile flower, the plant also has an antibacterial, anti-inflammatory and antioxidant effect!

Camomile

<u>Clover</u>

Most people have known what clover looks like since childhood. Supposedly, four-leaf clover is said to bring good luck and that is why the plant is very well known. Therefore, clover is very easy to recognise, even with the usual three leaves!

Clover leaves

The whole clover plant can be fed, both the flowers and the leaves and stems. In my experience, red clover is particularly popular.

Clover contains many valuable vitamins and minerals - from vitamin C, vitamin B1, vitamin B3 to calcium, magnesium, potassium and flavonoids. It is therefore an ideal food for rabbits!

Red clover with flowers

Cleaver / Bedstraw

Bedstraw is the generic term for many different special species of the same plant - probably best known are the burdock bedstraw and the meadow bedstraw.

You can find bedstraw all over the world. The plant is considered a natural remedy, as it contains valuable flavonoids and essential oils. The flavonoids strengthen the immune system of your rabbits. In addition, the ingredients of the bedstraw help against bacteria and viruses and the plant has a diuretic effect.

Ribwort Plantain

Ribwort plantain is also called a natural antibiotic. It is commonly known as a medicinal plant. The plantain family includes almost two hundred different species, but ribwort is usually the most common and relatively easy to find in most areas!

Leaves of ribwort plantain

The whole plant can be fed but most popular are usually the leaves. But you can also offer the flower and stem to your rabbits.

Ribwort plantain is rich in vitamin C, various B vitamins, zinc, potassium and silicic acid. The plant cleans the blood, inhibits inflammation and has an antibacterial effect. Therefore, this plant is a wonderful food for your animals!

In addition, ribwort plantain also has an antibiotic effect and is therefore often used for diseases and infections of the throat/pharynx/lung area. This is especially important for small animals, as colds can very quickly turn into deadly pneumonia - such infections are not to be trifled with in rabbits.

Ribwort Plantain Flower

Ground Ivy

The Ground Ivy plant belongs to the labiates. It provides high-quality bitter substances that support the metabolism and digestion of rabbits. Furthermore, Ground Ivy contains important essential oils, silicic acid, potassium and vitamin C. Ground Ivy also contains tanning agents which have an anti-inflammatory and antibacterial effect.

Ground Ivy loves humid climate and is mostly found on meadows, in embankments and in gardens. It is best to eat in a mixture but should not be fed in excessive amounts and should always be offered mixed with grass and other wild plants. Ground Ivy is a very good supplement, but not a primary food for rabbits.

Ground Ivy

St. John's Wort

St. John's Wort is a wonderful medicinal plant and is also used very often for humans. It not only calms the nerves and ensures a balanced and relaxed mind, but also cleans the blood, helps against inflammation and can even have an expectorant effect. Therefore St. John's Wort can also be used against colds.

Furthermore, St. John's Wort has an antibacterial and appetite-stimulating effect. It can help with cystitis as well as digestive problems and has antispasmodic and analgesic properties. All these positive properties of St. John's Wort make the plant an ideal feed to promote healthy rabbit nutrition.

St. John's Wort

There are so many wonderful wild plants that not all of them can be discussed in detail. I will certainly write a separate wild herb guide to do justice to all plants. Nevertheless, you will have noticed by now how many great plants nature offers our rabbits and that we can feed our little rascals with wild plants without any problems.

If you're still unsure about collecting food in the wild and don't feel comfortable identifying the plants, you can use a plant identification app. From my own experience I can recommend the app "Plantnet"! This is not paid advertising, but my own subjective opinion. The app is helpful and, in most cases, reliable. In the app you can take pictures of the plants and then you will be shown suggestions which plant it is. In most cases it works fine, but sometimes the results are not quite clear. If in doubt, leave the plant and ask a specialist first. Of course, you can also send me a photo of the plant and I will be happy to help you! You can find my email address in the legal notice at the end of this book!

Below is a list of other wild herbs that are popular with most rabbits:

- *Amaranth*

- *Dock*

- *White plantain*

- *Watercress*

- *Thistles (rabbits can tolerate the thorns)*

- *Veronica*

- *Cinquefoil*

- *Lady's mantle*

- *Goutweed*

- *Garlic mustard*

- *Marguerite*

- *Broadleaf plantain*

- *Rapeseed*

- *Marigold*

- *Sorrel*

- *Yarrow*

- *Celandine*

- *Chickweed*

- *Cranesbill / geranium*

- *Deadnettle*

- *Thyme*

- *Bird vetch*

Please do not feed the following plants (poisonous plants - list not exhaustive!)

- *Aloe*

- *Arum*

- *Christmas rose*

- *Ivy*

- *Monkshood*

- *Fern*

- *Foxglove*

- *Laburnum*

- *Autumn crocus / Meadow saffron*

(Deadly for rabbits and humans!)

- *Lilies*

- *Lily of the Valley (Deadly for rabbits and humans!)*

- *Oleander*

- *Delphinium*

- *Deadly nightshade / belladonna*

- *Solanum*

Trees: branches and leaves

Tree leaves and branches can wonderfully complement the feeding of grass, wild herbs and other leafy plants. Most native deciduous trees are suitable for feeding rabbits. In any case, there are countless tree species that can be fed without any problems and which are extremely healthy. A non-exhaustive list can be found at the end of this chapter. But first we want to take a closer look at the four tree species which, in my experience, are particularly good for rabbits!

<u>Oak</u>

The ingredients of oak have a digestive effect and help well with digestive problems, especially diarrhoea. As this is particularly important for rabbits and should always be well observed, it comes handy that oak can stimulate the digestive system and balance intestinal activity.

Oak

Beech

Beech tree leaves are very popular with rabbits. In my experience, the hornbeam is particularly popular. The beech tree can help against sniffles and other cold symptoms such as high temperature. That's why it is often used as a cold remedy, but it is also generally a wonderful food that can be fed daily.

Beech

Hazel

The leaves of the hazel are very easy to identify because of their distinctive shape and because they feel very 'soft'. They are not as 'hard' as the leaves of most other trees. You will certainly have noticed that there are red and green hazel trees - although the red hazel is admittedly more purple in colour. Both species are ideal for feeding. The hazel's ingredients have a particularly good effect on the liver and bile, but hazel can also have a healing effect on other organs as well.

Hazel

<u>Birch</u>

Birch trees can have a diuretic effect, just like wild herbs such as dandelion and nettle can, as described above. Birches can also help against inflammation.

Birch

Leaves and branches of other trees you can feed to your rabbits:

- *Apple tree*

- *Apricot tree*

- *Bamboo*

- *Pear tree*

- *Blackberry tree*

- *Fig tree*

- *Spruce*

- *Ginkgo*

- *Blueberry*

- *Raspberry*

- *Currant tree*

- *Pine*

- *Cherry tree*

- *Basswood*

- *Mirabelle*

- *Poplar*

- *Peach tree*

- *Plum tree*

- *Gooseberry*

- *Fir trees*

- *Willow*

- *Hawthorn*

Under no circumstances should you feed the following tree species (toxic!):

- *Boxwood*

- *Yew (Deadly!)*

- *Maikoa / Angel's trumpet*

- *Lucky bamboo (is not a real bamboo)*

- *Elderberry*

- *Laurel*

- *Magnolia*

- *Guelder rose / viburnum*

- *Castor / Palm of Christ*

Lettuce

Leafy vegetables are great food for rabbits, and lettuces are a very good supplement to meadow feeding. Many types of lettuce can be fed to rabbits without any doubt, and lettuce should be a large part of the diet if meadow feeding is not possible - or at least not always possible.

However, not all lettuce is the same. The varieties have very different advantages and disadvantages. In addition, not every type of lettuce is well suited to feeding, as some species provide hardly any nutrients. However, there are many types of lettuce that have a great added value for your rabbits.

By far the most suitable lettuces are the bitter lettuce varieties. The bitter substances contained in these lettuces are very healthy for rabbits - but also for humans. Many people don't like the bitter taste too much and therefore it is often covered up by dressings. However, it seems that rabbits are especially fond of bitter foods! This is also shown by the fact that almost all rabbits love bitter dandelion leaves.

Even in winter, lettuce feeding is usually possible without any problems. This comes especially handy, as it is known that in winter there is not much food to be found outside in nature. It is quite possible that you will have problems finding enough food for your rabbits in nature in winter. You can therefore choose from a variety of lettuces during the cold season.

The endive salad is typical and makes a great winter

lettuce. Other bitter lettuces such as radicchio, frisee and chicory are also very suitable and very nutritious. In my experience, radicchio is the most popular, but this can of course vary from rabbit to rabbit. Ideally, you always provide your animals with a selection of different foods.

Radicchio

Endive

The bitter substances in the lettuce varieties mentioned are very important for the digestion of your rabbits. They also have a positive effect on the liver function and on the bile. Furthermore, bitter substances can even alleviate pain and inhibit inflammation.

Rocket (although rocket is strictly speaking a cabbage), lollo rosso, lamb's lettuce and romaine lettuce are also great, healthy and delicious foods for your rabbits!

Lamb's lettuce

Apart from that, the majority of other types of lettuce are rather unsuitable for feeding rabbits - at least they should not be fed too often. This group includes iceberg lettuce and head/garden lettuce in particular. Unfortunately, these lettuces contain a lot of nitrate and a very low mineral content.

Arugula/Rocket

Free vegetable greens in the supermarket and at the weekly market

If you have ever looked around the weekly farmers market or supermarket, you have probably noticed that people usually leave or throw away the leafy parts of vegetables that can be used as food for rabbits!

Probably very few of you have ever eaten carrot leaves, kohlrabi leaves or cauliflower leaves. At least it is quite unusual. This is exactly what we as pet owners benefit from, because many people leave veggie leaves behind. Often there are even boxes in which the unneeded vegetable greenery can be put - and pet owners can then take it home with them!

Fortunately, leafy veggies are an ideal food for rabbits. In many supermarkets, you can take left-over leaves home free of charge. In addition, the retailers do not have to dispose of it - it is a win-win situation for everyone!

Of course, you should first ask whether it is okay to take the leaves with you, however, I have not yet seen this to be a problem. Usually, supermarkets are quite grateful for this "disposal method". This reduces food waste and also benefits your wallet.

I can particularly recommend the following veggie leaves:

- Kohlrabi leaves

- Carrot leaves

- Cauliflower leaves

- Radish leaves

- Celery leaves

Cabbage

There is a widespread myth that cabbage should not be fed to rabbits because it bloats. And yet it is so well suited to feeding rabbits in winter! If you don't find too many wild plants, grass, etc. in nature in winter, your rabbits' diet can be based on bitter salads and cabbage!

When fed properly, cabbage does not cause gas or other digestive problems. Such problems only occur if a rabbit is fed the wrong food and therefore already has a sick digestive tract. If a rabbit is given dry food (pellets or industrial (cereal) dry food) in addition to cabbage, it is possible that this is not compatible with feeding cabbage. Dry food is completely unnatural and therefore superfluous. If your rabbits are currently being fed dry food, it is best to slowly stop this way of feeding and then wait about two weeks before offering them some cabbage. During these two weeks, the digestive tract has time to regulate itself and regain its balance.

Furthermore, cabbage should be fed slowly in the beginning. This applies to any new food anyway. If changes in feeding take place too quickly, the digestive system will not have enough time to get used to the new food. Rabbits are much more sensitive than humans. Therefore, you should let your rabbit eat only a little cabbage out of your hand at the beginning and increase the amount daily. You will observe daily if there are changes in the rabbit's excrement or if the rabbit reacts negatively to the new food in any other way.

It is also essential that your rabbits get enough exercise. In humans, too, sufficient exercise is very important for an intact digestion - it is no different with rabbits. It is therefore important that your rabbits have enough room to run around and that they don't get bored.

Nevertheless, it must be said that not all cabbages are the same. Some types of cabbage have a relatively high proportion of high molecular weight carbohydrates. And what does that mean? High-molecular carbohydrates can actually promote gassing if they are eaten in excessive amounts or if a rabbit has a particularly sensitive digestive system. Therefore, these types of carbohydrates should not be offered in unlimited quantities but eaten in moderation. These are savoy cabbage, white cabbage, red cabbage and Brussels sprouts.

With the other types of cabbage, you don't have to worry about the quantities, but you can let your rabbits eat as much as they want - once they are used to the type of cabbage. In my experience, kale (one of the healthiest foods in the world for humans and rabbits!) and kohlrabi are particularly popular. However, cabbage varieties such as Chinese cabbage, broccoli, cauliflower and pak choi are also popular.

Other vegetables

There are many other vegetables that can be a wonderful addition to your rabbit's diet. How many other vegetables you feed to your rabbits depends on how much grass, wild herbs, leaves, lettuce and cabbage you can offer your animals - and how often you have the opportunity to do so. There are many rabbit owners who feed their animals almost all year round exclusively from plants found in nature. This is the most species-appropriate diet and comes closest to the diet of rabbits in the wild. But if and how much you can collect depends of course on the area you live in and on how much time you have.

Maybe you can find enough grass in your area and a few different wild herbs - that's a great basis! If you cannot offer a wide selection, you should add lettuces, cabbage and other vegetables so that your rabbits can choose from a wide variety. This will also help your rabbits to select the foods their bodies request and need.

So, let's take a closer look at some of the most common vegetables!

Fennel

Fennel can be a great help with stomach-ache. As a child, you might have been given fennel tea for stomach aches and pains, and perhaps you still associate this tea with a soothing effect on digestion. And rightly so! Not only does fennel work very well for humans, but also for rabbits. The taste of fresh fennel can be too intense for some people, but most rabbits love it. It is an ideal food supplement that can be offered regularly. However, fennel should not be the main food.

Fennel

Peppers

Peppers are a real vitamin C bomb! All kinds of peppers can be fed. You can also feed the inner white part and the seeds to your animals - even if humans usually cut this part away. Only the green part of peppers should not be offered to your rabbits, as it contains a lot of solanine. This is poisonous. Under normal circumstances rodents do not touch the stalk anyway. Either it does not taste good or the animals intuitively know that the stalk is not food! As a precaution, it is best not to offer it at all.

Red and yellow peppers

Tomatoes

All tomato varieties can be fed to rabbits. Ideally, however, you should not offer tomatoes on a daily basis and only give your animals small amounts, as tomatoes (similar to apples) are quite acidic. If a rabbit eats too much acidic food, this can favour orf (sore mouth infection). With orf, you should avoid all acidic fruits and vegetables until it is cured - and even then, you should only offer these foods in moderation. You should also remove the green stalks from the tomatoes before feeding them, as this contains a lot of solanine (similar to the green stalk of peppers) and is therefore toxic. If you keep this in mind, there should be no problems and you can offer your animals tomatoes from time to time.

Tomatoes

Carrots

Carrots are considered THE food for rabbits. Why is that? Because of Bugs Bunny chewing on a carrot all the time? Well, carrots are perfectly fine for rabbits now and then, but they should not make the main food!

As we now know, rabbits feed mainly on leafy and very high fibre food. Carrots are a tuberous vegetable and, unlike grasses, leaves, herbs, etc., they have a fairly high energy density; that means many calories. Carrots should therefore only be offered as a side dish.

Have you ever seen your animals nibble off small pieces of a carrot and spit them out again immediately? A relatively large number of animals do this. The reason for this is quite simple: sometimes the skin of the carrot does not taste good, and it is nibbled off and 'discarded' to get to the sweeter core of the carrot! Such behaviour is therefore no cause for concern.

Cucumber

Cucumbers are a great refreshment especially in summer and a great water supplier when rabbits have an increased need for water. Since cucumbers consist almost exclusively of water and provide hardly any nutrients, they should not be fed in too large quantities and should not be one of the main feeds.

It is not uncommon for rabbits to like only the skin of the cucumber and chew it all around. The inner part of the cucumber is then left lying around. This is a waste of food, but very normal behaviour. Especially with cucumbers, you should make sure that they are of organic quality, because the skins very often contain pesticides.

As mentioned before, cucumbers can be a great way to cool down in summer. To offer your rabbits a little fun at the same time, you can cut the cucumber into slices and then put them in a shallow water bath.

From this water bath the animals can fish the cucumber slices out. This provides inner and outer cooling and a little fun. The high-water content of this vegetable prevents dehydration of your rabbits in hot summer months!

Cucumber

The following vegetables are not suitable as rabbit food:

- Avocados (is actually a berry; may be poisonous and much too fatty)

- Mushrooms (are strictly speaking not vegetables, but fungi)

- Chilli (too spicy)

- Potatoes (also no potato skins!)

- Horseradish (too spicy)

- Olives (especially not pickled ones!)

- Radishes (too spicy)

- Rhubarb

- Onions (too spicy)

Treats

Of course, we should feed our rabbits in a healthy way and appropriate to their species. They get lots of hay, wild herbs, grasses, leaves, twigs, leafy vegetables, cabbage, bitter lettuces ... But who of you nibbles some treats from time to time? You treat yourself to a chocolate bar, a bowl of chips, a few cookies. That is why you can treat your rabbits to something once in a while! No rabbit will get sick if it gets a treat from time to time - and mental health should be taken care of as well.

However, you should make sure that the treats are as healthy and natural as possible. Yoghurt drops, for example, have no place in a rabbit's tummy. Very healthy and tasty snacks are pea flakes and sunflower seeds!

Sunflower seeds are a wholefood, as they occur in their original form in nature and are not industrially processed. They provide your rabbits with lots of vitamin E, B1, B3, B6, zinc, iron and magnesium. Although rabbits are leaf eaters and not seed eaters, the kernels are ideal as a treat. They are also effective against dry skin and keep it supple.

However, it should also be noted that sunflower seeds are very rich in fat and can therefore make one overweight if eaten in excess. You should never offer treats in a bowl, as rabbits will probably overeat on the treats. A treat should remain something special and should therefore only be fed from your hand!

Feeding out of the hand can strengthen the connection between you and your rabbits and can also promote communication. For example, you can teach your rabbits little tricks to show you when they want a treat.

For example, hold a sunflower seed over your pet's head or nose so that it has to stand on its hind legs to get the treat. You can also slowly move your hand around the animal so that it has to turn on its own axis to get the treat. After a while, your rabbit will remember what it has to do to get the treat. Then it will come to you, turn around or stand on its hind legs - and ask for a little treat.

Besides sunflower seeds, pea flakes are also extremely popular with rabbits! These flakes are made from 100% dried peas, which are pressed into flakes after drying. No unhealthy additives are added.

Although peas are not an unhealthy food, it should be remembered that rabbits in the wild naturally feed on extremely watery foods. These provide few calories. This means that pea flakes are kind of a calorie bomb for rabbits - for this reason, they should of course only be offered in moderation and only be fed from the hand so that this treat remains something special for the rabbit to look forward to.

Pea flakes are to rabbits what chocolate and crisps are to humans. Compared to fresh green food, pea flakes are rich in calories, but at the same time they provide valuable minerals and vitamins (iron, zinc, calcium, folic acid, magnesium, vitamins K, E, C and A as well as B vitamins).

In addition, you can also offer your rabbits the following treats:

- Apple pieces

- Banana pieces

- Blueberries

- Blackberries

- Raspberries

- Cranberries

- Grapes

- Pumpkin seeds

- Linseed

Pellets and (cereal) dried fodder

Let us now talk about the most common mistake made in caring for rabbits: Feeding pellets and/or (grain) dry food. Please do not blame yourself if you too have been feeding your rabbits dry food. Unfortunately, this type of feeding is still often recommended nowadays, especially in inferior guidebooks and pet shops.

Unfortunately, this type of food is not appropriate for the species and very often causes many diseases. Especially often the digestive tract gets sick and dental problems occur, because there is not enough chewing for the necessary tooth abrasion.

One could possibly assume that hard pellets and other hard dry food are well suited for tooth abrasion, but this is a fallacy. The opposite is the case. Dry food softens quickly when it comes into contact with saliva and does not need to be chewed long and well. Grasses, hay and other raw fibre-rich foods must be chewed very thoroughly and for a long time, which is essential for an intact and healthy dentition. The teeth do not primarily rub against the food, but against each other! Due to the intensive and constant grinding and crushing, the teeth of the upper dentition constantly rub against the teeth of the lower dentition and vice versa. In this way the teeth are well and evenly 'filed'!

In addition, industrial dry food swells up a lot. This is not at all good for rabbit digestion, partly because the rabbit is satiated for a long time and eats less green fodder than it would under normal circumstances. Unfortunately, dental and/or digestive problems caused by industrial dried fodder are also the reason why so many rabbits pass away prematurely.

Our domestic rabbits still have the same digestive system as wild rabbits. Wild rabbits naturally do not eat dry food, but feed on green plants growing in nature. We have already discussed this before. For this reason, your rabbits' diet should be based on the food they would find and eat in the wild.

Even if the rabbit's body *can* process this type of processed/industrial food, that does not mean that it *should*. Rabbits are not physiologically designed for that.

You can compare this to human nutrition: while a rabbit is physiologically a herbivore, a human being is physiologically a frugivore. The natural diet of humans is based on fruits, nuts, vegetables, wholemeal foods, legumes and the like. In order to determine the natural form of nutrition of a living being, the dentition and the digestive tract are considered in particular. The utilisation of certain ingredients is also included in the definition - while the cholesterol contained in meat, for example, is harmful to humans, it has no negative effect on, for example, lions and cats, which are carnivores from a physiological point of view.

The basis of the herbivorous diet is leaves, grasses, wild herbs, leafy vegetables and the like. However, if a rabbit is fed a different diet, the risk of disease and mortality increases. This applies equally to all living creatures.

If you look at the list of ingredients of some food manufacturers, you may be shocked. Very often the first ingredient is "grain/cereal" (this includes for example oats, barley, corn, wheat). None of this belongs in the small rabbit tummy and you should definitely avoid such food!

But the other ingredients are also a cause for concern. Mostly "vegetable by-products" are listed. This can mean everything and nothing. "By-products" is simply a euphemism for "waste". And that is no joke. The industry sees such by-products as waste that either has to be disposed of or can be 'recycled' to generate further profit. So, it is simply mixed into rabbit feed.

Furthermore, industrial dried fodder often contains "oils and fats". You know that rabbits feed on green plants - there is no oil or fat worth mentioning in them. The crowning point is that it is not even specified that vegetable fats must be used. The manufacturers are even allowed to mix in animal fats and thus turn your rabbits into carnivores!

It is also worth mentioning that your rabbits will probably drink very little water if they are fed a diet appropriate to their species. If animals feed on green plants, they usually take in a lot of water already through the food. Thirst is very rare with a species-appropriate diet. If your rabbits are given dry food, they will have to drink a lot more to prevent dehydration. Nevertheless, you should always offer your rabbits fresh water, especially on warm summer days, even if they are being fed properly.

First time feeding and change of diet

Please note that each new food should be fed slowly in the beginning. This is especially true if your rabbits have been fed dry food up to now; however, even animals that have already been fed properly should be slowly accustomed to new vegetables, new leaf types, new wild herbs, etc. You should always keep a close eye on your rabbits to see if the acclimatisation or habituation is happening at the right pace.

Moreover, pellets and other dry food should not be struck off the list from one day to the next as this would be too rapid a changeover. Administer less dry food to your animals from day to day, until after one or two weeks you no longer offer any. This does not apply to hay, of course, because hay should always be given at least as an additional option to fresh greens.

When you offer a new food for the first time, you should start with small amounts. First give your rabbits a fingernail-sized piece of a new vegetable, a leaf of a new tree species, a few stalks of grass, etc. - so that the sensitive rabbit digestion can get used to the new food. Otherwise, digestive problems could possibly occur. The human body is much more robust than the small rabbit body. While humans can cope with almost any new food immediately, rabbits first have to get used to new food. Depending on the rabbit, this can take some time and that's perfectly fine. Besides, not every rabbit is the same - some are more sensitive, some take their time. This is also perfectly ok.

These aspects are also important when winter is approaching. In the cold season, you can either not find any grass, wild plants or other leaves outside - or at least you won't find as much as in the warmer seasons. There are some herbs that are usually persistent even in winter. These include dandelion, daisies and ribwort. Grass can also still be found in many areas. If you have the opportunity, you should therefore feed small amounts of plants from nature even in winter, so that your rabbits do not completely wean themselves.

If you do not have access to plants in the wild during the cold season, that is fine. You can get through the winter with cabbage, bitter lettuces, leaves and other vegetables. However, you should remember to start feeding all wild plants, tree leaves and grasses 'slowly' in the spring, as the rabbit's digestion will probably have 'forgotten' these foods and will have to get used to the change of diet again.

Note from the author

I very much hope that the tips and explanations in this guide have helped you. Rabbits are extremely special creatures, very different from the species "human". Therefore, it is important to know what our rabbits' needs are so that we can respond to them in the best possible way and make them happy all round!

If you have any further questions or concerns, please feel free to contact me via email. You can find my email address in the following legal notice. I am always happy to help you!

Finally, dear reader: product reviews are the basis for the success of independent authors. For this reason, I would be very grateful for feedback on this guide in the form of a review. Please let me know in your review how you liked the book. If you do not have time for providing a review, you can alternatively just award stars without writing a written statement. A few words would be great, of course. But no matter if it's long or short: with your opinion or your star rating you help future readers as well as me as an author! Thank you so much.

I wish you (and your bunnies) all the best and lots of fun exploring food options. Stay happy and healthy - and enjoy your time together!

Imprint

Title of the book: Bunny Tummy – Species appropriate rabbit nutrition – A comprehensive guide to rabbit food and how to reduce your costs

Author: Alina Daria Djavidrad

Contact: Wiesenstr. 6, 45964 Gladbeck, Germany

Email: info@simple-logic.net

Web: https://www.simple-logic.net

1st edition (2020)

Printed in Great Britain
by Amazon